Conquering Social Anxiety

A Practical Guide to Overcoming Social Anxiety and Building Self-Esteem

Chloe B. Johnson

The information contained in this book is not intended to replace any treatment. It is still best to seek professional help. This book is only a supplement. The information contained in this book is accurate. It is a product of extensive research. This book was written to the best of the author's knowledge. But the author should not be held liable for omissions and errors. The photos in this book are taken from stock photo websites.

Upon reading this book, you agree to hold the author harmless against and from any costs or damages that can result from the application of the information provided by this book. This disclaimer applies to any direct or indirect injury or damages caused by the use of the information in this book, whether it's a tort, negligence, contract, or any other cause of legal action.

You agree to accept all the risks of applying the information contained in this book. If needed, consult a doctor to ensure that you're healthy and capable enough to apply and use the strategies presented in this book.

DEDICATION

To all those who struggle with social anxiety, you are not alone. This book is dedicated to empowering you with the tools and understanding to overcome your fears and live the life you deserve.

WHAT'S NEXT

You will enjoy reading this book, and I am confident that you will find it speaks deep into your soul. You can find more information on my books and myself personally. Go to https://jestmy.com/r/chloebooks

FREE GIFT

Firstly, I want to thank you for making my journey a part of your incredible journey. Studies have shown that most adults find it hard to self-improve but can significantly improve by simply making use of a journal to track and support their progress. So, I have decided to offer you a FREE print at-home wellness journal. This journal contains eight different methods to assist you in superior wellness. Download your free gift now.
https://jestmy.com/r/chloegift

SUPPORT GROUPS

Studies have shown that parallel to journaling and tracking your progress and feelings, sharing your story and hearing others tell their story has an incredibly positive impact on people. So, I have started a group for like-minded people. If you are looking for a group of incredible people who share your experiences and have similar journeys and would like to share your story, you must join our group today at:
https://jestmy.com/r/chloegroup

CONTENTS

Table of Contents

INTRODUCTION

Social anxiety is a type of anxiety that causes you to feel shy, embarrassed, and self-conscious in social situations. It's different from regular nervousness because it affects your ability to function normally in everyday life; for example, you might have trouble making eye contact with people or speaking up at meetings. Social anxiety can also lead to depression and substance abuse because these may help mask feelings of low self-worth.

What is social anxiety?

Social anxiety is a fear of being judged by others. Social situations can make you feel embarrassed or nervous, and you may be afraid that other people will judge you for your actions, appearance, or behavior.

For example:

You get anxious in social situations, such as meeting new people or when you have to talk to colleagues at work.

You worry about doing something wrong in front of other people and feeling embarrassed. For example, maybe someone notices that your clothes are mismatched or that there's food stuck between your teeth during lunch with co-workers at the office cafeteria!

You find it hard to relax and enjoy yourself when out with friends because of this fear of being embarrassed by others' reactions to what you say or do (or don't say).

How does it manifest?

Social anxiety manifests in several different ways. The most common physical symptoms include rapid heartbeat, blushing, shortness of breath and nausea.

Behavioral symptoms can include avoiding social situations, having to prepare ahead of time for conversations with others (e.g., coming up with good icebreakers), being unable to communicate your thoughts or emotions verbally and feeling uncomfortable when you're around people who are talking about themselves.

Causes of social anxiety.

Social anxiety may be caused by genetics. If your parents or siblings have anxiety disorders, you're more likely to develop one yourself.

Social anxiety can also be a response to trauma and other negative experiences in your life or past. This might include bullying, being teased, or experiencing abuse at home or school as a child.

Environmental factors also play a role in social anxiety disorder development: for example, if you live in an area where there aren't many people around who are similar to you (such as living out in the country), it can make it difficult for someone with social phobia because they don't have access to anyone they know well enough yet who can help them feel comfortable going outside of their comfort zone when it comes time for them

Where to get help.

If talking to a therapist or joining a support group isn't an option, there are still ways to get help. Many people find that reading self-help books and practicing meditation can be beneficial. If you're looking for information on how to practice meditation, try Google or YouTube. There are thousands of videos with instructions on how to meditate, as well as guided meditations that you can listen to while sitting comfortably in your home!

If all else fails, don't give up hope! Even if nothing seems to be working right now and the symptoms of social anxiety aren't subsiding, know that it will eventually go away - and if not by itself then with treatment from a medical professional (which may include medication).

How to overcome social anxiety?

The first step to overcoming social anxiety is to determine your triggers. A lot of people are afraid of public speaking or talking in front of other people. Other people tend to become nervous when they're around their peers or family members, but not strangers. If you're someone who struggles with social anxiety, take some time to think about what situations make you nervous and create a list of them. Then, prioritize this list based on how frequently they occur in your life and how much they affect your quality of life overall. This will help give you an idea as to what needs addressing first when it comes time for treatment!

Once you have an idea about where the treatment needs focusing (and there may be several areas), then it's time for some research! Try reading up on different methods used by professionals who specialize in helping individuals overcome social anxiety disorder (SAD). Try looking online at university websites where researchers have published articles about their work with SAD patients - some universities even have specific programs dedicated solely towards treating SAD patients! With so many options available today, thanks largely due to credit card companies that provide zero-interest financing options on purchases made within a certain time frame from the purchase date; there really isn't any reason why anyone should despair overpaying off debt such as credit cards/loans after college graduation day arrives."

Overcoming social anxiety and shyness.

Social anxiety can be a difficult condition to overcome, but it is possible. If you are struggling with social anxiety or shyness and want to start overcoming it, there are some simple steps you can take that will help you on your journey.

Recognize where your social anxiety comes from. To overcome this condition, you need to know what it is that triggers that feeling of dread in certain situations. For example: do you get nervous when talking with strangers? Or are those butterflies more about being put on the spot for an impromptu presentation? Knowing what makes your heart race will help give focus to work ahead; this way, when a situation arises where these feelings crop up again (and they probably will), you'll know exactly how to respond. Additionally, understanding why this fear manifests itself in such specific ways can be helpful in overcoming it entirely - the better we understand ourselves as human beings, after all!

Social anxiety is a real problem for many people, and it can be difficult to know what to do about it. When you're feeling anxious in social situations, your mind is full of thoughts that make you feel even more nervous. The good news is that there are ways you can help yourself overcome this problem! We hope this chapter was helpful in giving some insight into how social anxiety works, what causes it and where you can get help if need be.

DAILY SOCIAL ANXIETY STRATEGIES

If you suffer from social anxiety, there are some strategies that can help. We'll explore them below and explain how they're effective.

Focus on the positive

The best way to deal with social anxiety is to focus on the positive. Think about what you can do, rather than what you're worried about doing or not doing. What are your strengths? What can you do today that will make a difference in your life? How can you take advantage of the present moment?

And what's ahead for you in the future?

This isn't just a feel-good suggestion; research shows that taking an optimistic approach helps people overcome their fear of failure and rejection. For example, one study found that participants who were taught to think positively about their abilities were more likely than others to persist at an unsolvable task - and ultimately perform better as well!

Breathe with your belly

Breathing with your belly is a great way to take a break from your thoughts and focus on something other than anxiety.

Breathe in through your nose and out through your mouth.

Breathe deeply, filling up the bottom of your lungs first, then expanding into the rest of them as you breathe out slowly. If you're having trouble concentrating on breathing, try counting each breath until it gets easier for you to do this without thinking about it too much - it's best if you can get to 10 before having to think again!

You may need more than one session of breathing exercises like these throughout the day; every time I start finding myself feeling anxious or worried while socializing or working at home alone (or whatever else is making me feel self-conscious), I'll repeat my deep breaths until it feels better again!

Realise that you're not alone

The first thing to remember is that you are not alone. Everyone has some level of social anxiety, so don't let yourself feel like your problems are unique or special.

Even if you feel like you're suffering from a severe case of social anxiety, remember that plenty of people have it worse than you and still manage to go on and live their lives happily every day! You can do this too!

Stay in the moment

Staying in the present is easier said than done. It's easier to stay focused on what you're doing when your mind is racing with anxious thoughts and emotions. But if you can, stay focused on the task at hand. When it comes to social anxiety, this means not thinking about what happened in the past or what could happen in the future. Avoid worrying about how people perceive you based on body language or facial expressions; even if someone does think negatively about you, it won't change anything besides fueling your worry (which is something we'll talk about later).

Focus instead on being mindful of all your senses: sight, sound, and smell. For example, take a look around while having a conversation with someone and notice things like colour schemes or interesting wall art; listen attentively to what others have to say and make sure there aren't any background noises that may be distracting (iPhones are especially bad for this); smell some flowers before going into a meeting so that they'll be fresh in your mind when meeting new people later on down the road - it sounds silly, but it works!

Visualise a positive outcome

Visualisation is a powerful tool and can help you overcome your fears. When you visualise yourself as confident and calm, it helps to reinforce confidence in yourself, which supports the self-talk that you can do whatever it is that you need to do.

So how do you use visualisation? It's easy! Just close your eyes and imagine yourself in a situation that makes you anxious (e.g., giving a presentation). Visualise yourself being successful easily and confidently or feel like an expert who knows exactly what he/she is talking about. You may even want to create a whole movie screenplay for this event with happy endings for all involved!

Avoid overthinking

Humans are naturally self-doubting creatures. We second-guess our decisions and imagine how we could've done better in any given situation. This is called rumination, a form of overthinking that can lead to anxiety and stress. If you think about past mistakes or what might have been in your head instead of focusing on what's going on now, try catching yourself mid-thought and redirecting your attention back to whatever you're doing in the present moment (e.g., calling someone).

Question your anxious thoughts

A helpful question to ask yourself when experiencing social anxiety is: Is this thought useful? If not, don't believe it.

There are two critical points here. First, recognise that your thoughts and feelings about social situations are often hostile or scary. Second, do not take these thoughts and feelings as fact - they're just thoughts and feelings (and, in some cases, false ones). They aren't facts about the world around you or your place in it - they're just ideas from your brain at the moment. This can be hard to do because being anxious makes it seem like everything happening around us is somehow more important than what's happening inside us (e.g., "I'm so nervous right now!"). But if we're able to step back from our anxiety-ridden mindsets just long enough for them to pass through us, then we can see how much power they hold over us

Be aware of biased thinking patterns

Bias is a tendency to accept or reject claims based on partial and often misleading information. When it comes to social anxiety, biased thinking patterns can significantly impact how you react to social situations.

Bias is when you jump to conclusions about your actions, those of others, or the situation at hand (e.g., I'm such an idiot! Why did I say that? Everyone must think I'm stupid.). It's also making assumptions about why other people do what they do (e.g., He didn't respond because he thinks I'm boring). Bias occurs when we see things in black-and-white terms rather than shades of grey (e.g., "He was mean to me" vs "He didn't say anything nice").

Some bias may be rooted in reality; however, if not managed properly, it can lead down a path where you are catastrophising your mistakes and making assumptions about other people's intentions without evidence supporting them - two factors that will exacerbate your anxiety and make it more likely that anxiety-provoking situations will occur again in the future.

Practice being assertive

In the language of assertive communication, you're asserting yourself when you say no to something, ask for what you want or need, and stand up for yourself in any situation.

Being assertive doesn't mean being aggressive or rude; it means standing up for your rights while acknowledging the rights of others. It also means being honest with yourself and others when you feel upset and working through that feeling by talking about it openly.

Learning to be more assertive will help you build confidence in all areas of your life, especially when dealing with social anxiety. And since social anxiety often goes together with a fear of conflict and disagreement (which may lead us to avoid speaking up), practising assertiveness skills is vital!

Let go of "should" statements.

In this section, we'll talk about the concept of "should." We'll discuss how to let go of it, use it to your advantage, and not let it control you.

Should statements be an automatic response to social situations? When you feel anxiety about a problem or interaction with others, your brain may give you a "should" statement to try to make sense of what's happening.

For example:

I should have said something when they were talking about their vacation plans! It would have made me sound more interested if I had talked about going skiing on my trip last winter!

But now they're leaving, and I'm alone again...

It's essential to be aware that these thoughts are just there for comfort - they're not necessarily true - and that kindness is better than beating yourself up. If you can recognise these statements for what they are (anxiety-provoking), then you can use them as fuel for a change instead of letting them control how you see yourself or your life. If someone asks how much money someone else makes and then thinks, "I should earn at least two times as much," try thinking instead: Well...maybe my work is more important than theirs?

Fake it till you make it

In mental health, it's a common phrase to "fake it till you make it." In other words, if you act like you're confident and sure of yourself, your brain will eventually begin to believe that that's who you indeed are. This is why people sometimes go through periods where they feel like they're not good enough or smart enough, or pretty enough - because their brains aren't used to being told otherwise.

One way I've found that helps me manage my social anxiety is by constantly reminding myself of one thing: everyone makes mistakes, feels vulnerable at some point, and has certain parts of themselves that they hide from others. We all have things about ourselves we don't want others to see, but most people are so afraid of being rejected because of these things that they never let anyone else in close enough to see them anyway!

So instead of trying so hard not to mess up or say something embarrassing in front of someone else (which can be more stressful than just doing those things), remind yourself that no one expects perfection out there. Everyone understands how difficult social situations can be (especially if they've ever talked with someone with SAD). Instead, focus on showing your true self while getting help when needed: ask questions when uncertain; ask for advice when unsure what direction would work best; ask someone nearby if he needs help finding something he dropped on accident (or whatever).

Practice mindful meditation

Mindfulness meditation can also help reduce anxiety by increasing your awareness of the present moment. By focusing on your breath, you're practising being in the moment and not worrying about other things. It's a great way to train yourself in non-judgmental awareness and acceptance of life as it is right now. Daily Social Anxiety Strategies, many effective strategies to overcome social anxiety and shyness, tips for long-term social success

Focus on the positive

The first step in overcoming social anxiety is to change your mindset. Focus on the positive aspects of your life and be proud of what you've accomplished so far. You're in control of your life, so it's essential to appreciate this fact and use it as motivation for achieving long-term success in social situations.

Breathe with your belly

When you feel anxious about interacting with others, breathing can help calm you down because it forces you to focus on the present moment instead of worrying about how things will turn out later or feeling self-conscious about how people around you perceive you at that very moment (which can lead them feeling more anxious too). Take a deep breath through your nose while pushing out any air from inside your chest as if trying not let anything escape; then allow all air to flow back into both nostrils before exhaling again through both nostrils slowly like an underwater swimmer coming up towards surface level where there's plenty oxygen available! This simple trick works wonders because it quickly distracts attention away from negative thoughts towards something tangible like physical sensation, which makes sense when we're talking about breathing technique but also gives us time to think things over calmly before engaging socially again...

I hope this chapter has given you some ideas on overcoming social anxiety. It can be a difficult journey, but one that is worth it in the end. Remember that everyone must start somewhere and that even small steps towards overcoming any fear are still steps forward. Practice these strategies daily until they become second nature for you!

HOW SOCIAL ANXIETY DISORDER AFFECTS RELATIONSHIPS

Social anxiety disorder (SAD) is a mental health condition that can make it hard for people to interact with others. The symptoms of SAD can range from mild to severe, and they're often triggered by fear of being judged or criticised in social situations. If you have a social anxiety disorder, it can impact your relationships at home, work, or school. In this chapter, we'll discuss how SAD affects relationships and offer strategies for overcoming it.

How does Social Anxiety Disorder (SAD) affect relationships?

Social Anxiety Disorder (SAD) is an anxiety disorder that can cause significant distress and impairment in social, occupational, and other vital areas of functioning. It often occurs with other anxiety disorders in what is referred to as comorbidities. For example, SAD patients may also experience panic disorder or generalised anxiety disorder. This can make a recovery more difficult because each condition requires specialised treatment.

If you have SAD, it means you're concerned about being judged by others based on your performance in social situations like parties or interviews. You may feel anxious and uncomfortable around unfamiliar people or even close friends if they're watching you closely or criticising your behavior. In severe cases where these fears come true all the time (rather than just occasionally), it might be time to seek help from a therapist who specializes in dealing with this specific problem

Avoidance of conflict can cause stress in a relationship.

Avoiding conflict can be a red flag for social anxiety disorder. If you find yourself avoiding conflict in your relationship, it may mean that your partner is getting frustrated with your behavior. For example, imagine you avoid an argument with your partner about something that bothers them. Your partner may become angry or upset, but because you don't want to challenge him or her, you won't address their feelings directly. This avoidance of conflict can lead to resentment on both ends - and eventually lead to depression and anxiety as well as loss of trust in the relationship.

Disagreements and arguments are avoided because of fears of rejection.

Social anxiety disorder often makes it difficult for you to express your anger toward someone. You may avoid disagreements and arguments altogether because you fear being rejected or judged if the disagreement turns into an argument. You may also feel that it's not okay to be angry with someone else, especially in front of other people.

When your partner asks you what's wrong or why they did something that upset you, it can be difficult for someone with social anxiety disorder to explain how they feel about what happened. This can lead your partner to assume that nothing is wrong or that there are no valid reasons for feeling hurt by their actions.

One or both partners may feel that they must put on an act around each other.

It's common for one or both partners to feel that they must put on an act around each other. This can lead to stress and resentment, anger, depression, and isolation.

Intimate relationships may be avoided at all costs.

It's common for someone with social anxiety disorder to avoid intimate relationships at all costs. Those with SAD are afraid of being judged or rejected and may also fear that others will see them as weak or inferior. They may be so scared of rejection that they'll do anything possible to avoid getting close to anyone - including family members! This can lead to an incredibly lonely life because it cuts off a source of support: having people around who understand you and love you unconditionally.

Partners may feel like they're walking on eggshells around each other.

If you have social anxiety, it can be hard to tell when your partner is angry or upset. You're more likely to avoid conflict than confront it head-on. This can cause stress in a relationship as partners feel like they're walking on eggshells around each other - tiptoeing their way through life together rather than being able to openly discuss their feelings with one another. Partners may also feel like they're not good enough because of the impact of social anxiety disorder on the relationship

Self-doubt and self-criticism are common with SAD.

It's important to note that with social anxiety disorder, self-doubt and self-criticism are common. When you start comparing yourself unfavorably to others, it can seem like there is no way for you to win. If you don't think people will like your chapter on Facebook or Instagram, then why should they even care about what you have to say?

It's also important because this kind of thinking can lead to depression - and depression can lead back into the cycle of negative thoughts about oneself and constant self-doubt.

SAD symptoms can increase depression, anxiety, and loneliness.

If you have social anxiety disorder, you might experience depression and loneliness. In turn, these can make your social anxiety worse. This is called a vicious cycle because it keeps going in circles.

If you have depression or loneliness because of SAD, it's important to seek help from a mental health professional as soon as possible. The longer these feelings go untreated, the more difficult they are to get rid of and prevent their recurrence once treated properly.

Our ability to cope with social situations can decrease over time when we don't engage in the outside world.

As you avoid social situations, your ability to cope with them decreases over time. The more you avoid social situations, the less you practice being in them. As a result, it eventually becomes harder for you to feel comfortable engaging with other people. Your self-confidence also decreases: if someone has trouble engaging in conversation with their friends and family members, it's easy for them to think that there must be something wrong with them or that they're not as good as other people. When this happens often enough, our sense of belonging begins to wane too - we can start feeling like strangers even when we know our loved ones very well (or even when they're trying to help us through a difficult moment).

Being open and honest with your partner about your fears is a sign of strength and bravery rather than weakness or cowardice.

The next step is to open and be honest with your partner about what's going on. This can be a little scary, but it's far better than the alternative of keeping your feelings and emotions bottled up, which will only serve to make things worse.

Being open and honest with your partner about your fears is a sign of strength and bravery rather than weakness or cowardice. If you don't communicate, they'll feel like their opinion doesn't matter to you - and if they're not important enough for you to bother communicating with them, then why should they care about the relationship?

If this seems too overwhelming or difficult, consider talking it over in therapy before approaching them directly (you might even have someone who specializes in relationships).

Sometimes it helps to remind ourselves that we really do want to face our fears so we're not leaving our partner feeling like they're constantly being shut out.

It can be hard to tell your partner about your fears, especially if you're not sure that they won't think less of you. But sometimes the best way to deal with social anxiety is being honest about it. Not only does this show that you're willing to face your fears, but it also demonstrates strength.

Someone who's afraid of spiders is strong enough to admit that they're afraid of spiders; someone who doesn't want to go on a date is strong enough to say "no"; and someone who wants to spend time with her partner but worries she'll embarrass herself is strong enough to ask for help before turning down an invitation.

Partners often aren't aware of how their behavior affects us because we try so hard not show them how we feel or what we need - and then when something goes wrong in our relationship, we blame ourselves (or assume they do). If you're struggling with social anxiety disorder as well as having a relationship, try talking openly and honestly with your partner about what makes things difficult for both of you: don't assume anything!

If you're living with Social Anxiety Disorder (SAD), you may have noticed that your relationship is suffering because of it. But don't worry, there are ways to overcome this condition and get back to a healthy, happy relationship. Don't give up hope!

SOCIAL ANXIETY IS NOT AN UNFIXABLE CONDITION

Social anxiety is a condition that can affect anyone. It's not an uncommon problem, and it's not something that you have to feel ashamed of. In fact, social anxiety is highly treatable! There are many different approaches to treating this condition, and there are also many ways to overcome your social anxiety so that you can be more comfortable in social situations. This chapter will discuss the causes of social anxiety, what the signs are for someone who suffers from this condition, and how you can get help from your doctor if you think you may have a problem with social anxiety.

Social anxiety can be caused in many ways.

Social anxiety can be caused by many factors. It is not uncommon for people who suffer from social anxiety to have a genetic predisposition for it. This means that the condition can run in families and is passed down from generation to generation. Other times, people may have had traumatic experiences as a child that caused them to develop this condition later in life. If your parents were not supportive, or if you were bullied during school, then it's possible that this may have led to social anxiety being triggered at some point in your life (though this does not happen with everyone).

If you're wondering how long social anxiety lasts for and what causes it, we've got answers for those questions too!

Social anxiety is a condition that can be fixed and treated.

The first step to overcoming social anxiety is understanding that this condition is not an unfixable condition. You can overcome your social anxiety, but you need the right tools to do so. The next section will cover some of those tools, including therapy and medication as ways to treat social anxiety.

What are the signs of social anxiety?

The signs of social anxiety are many and varied. Here are some common ones:

Avoidance. The first thing you'll notice if you have social anxiety is that you avoid the situations that cause it, such as big parties or class presentations.

Fear of judgment and embarrassment. Many people with social anxiety are afraid they will be judged negatively by others and that they will embarrass themselves in front of others, possibly causing them to lose control or make fools of themselves.

Feeling like you're being always watched and under constant scrutiny from others, even when no one else is around (it's called an "out-of-body" sensation). This can cause severe panic attacks when it happens while interacting with others because they might think you're acting strangely if they notice your body movements or facial expressions; this causes more embarrassment and increases the cycle further until something breaks it…

How do you deal with social anxiety?

Some people use medication to help them deal with anxiety. These medications can be a good way to start working on your social anxiety, especially if you have a more severe case of it. However, these drugs are only meant for short-term use and shouldn't be used for years at a time.

There are also many different types of therapy that can help reduce your symptoms of social anxiety, including cognitive behavioral therapy (CBT) and acceptance and commitment therapy (ACT). These therapies involve learning how to change your thought patterns about yourself or the world around you so that they don't make you feel anxious anymore.

Self-help books are another option; there are many books available online which provide tips on how to overcome social anxiety or teach relaxation exercises that can help reduce stress levels associated with the condition. Social anxiety can be overcome through quick and easy treatment options. Anxiety disorders are among the most common mental health conditions in the United States. According to the Anxiety and Depression Association of America (ADAA), anxiety disorders are highly treatable, with an estimated 80% of people with an anxiety disorder receiving some form of treatment. Social anxiety is a type of phobia characterized by fear and avoidance of social situations due to fear that you will be judged by others or embarrassed in public. It is one of the most common psychological problems, affecting between 3%-13% of the population at any given time; it occurs three times more often in women than men.

Treatment options for social anxiety include medications such as antidepressants and anti-anxiety drugs as well as certain types of therapy such as cognitive behavioral therapy (CBT). CBT is a form of therapy that helps patients identify their negative thoughts and replace them with more positive ones, which over time can improve your outlook on life. Self-help techniques such as mindfulness meditation may also prove effective in treating this condition if taken seriously enough by those who wish to overcome their fears regarding interactions with others

In this chapter, we have discussed the causes of social anxiety, its symptoms and how to overcome it. We hope that you have found this valuable information useful and will be able to apply it in your life. If you are suffering from social anxiety or know someone who is, please do not hesitate to reach out for help!

OVERCOMING SOCIAL ANXIETY WHEN STARTING CONVERSATIONS

It's not easy to start a conversation with a stranger. And it's even more difficult when you suffer from social anxiety. But if you're like me, then you know that the best way to overcome your fear of talking to people is simply by doing it. And if you're thinking about making some new friends, here are 10 simple tips for overcoming your social anxiety and starting conversations with strangers:

Get clear on why you want to start a conversation.

If you're looking to start a conversation with a stranger, it's important to be clear on why you want to do that. Here are some good reasons:

To practice your social skills

To meet new people

To make friends

To feel confident in yourself

To be more outgoing or extroverted

Know when it's likely to be easy to start a conversation.

When they're alone. If you see someone sitting by themselves, or if they're standing at a table waiting for food and have no one in their group with them, this is an excellent time to strike up a conversation.

When they're reading a book or another type of media that requires concentration. In this case, it doesn't matter what kind of book or magazine - it's just the fact that they're focused on the material that makes it easier to start talking. You can even say something like "You look like you're really into that; what are you reading?"

When there's clearly nothing else going on around them (i.e., when there are no other distractions). Therefore train stations and bus stop sometimes work so well: because there aren't any other people around who could potentially be interrupting your conversation as soon as it starts up again!

Be mindful of your body language.

Body language is a great way to start a conversation. You can use it to show interest in the other person, show that you're confident and make yourself more approachable. If you feel nervous about approaching someone, try standing with your chest puffed out, shoulders back and head high. This will help you feel more confident and give off an air of confidence that should make approaching others easier for you.

If there's something interesting around (e.g., an interesting painting), make sure to point it out before saying anything else! The mutual appreciation of art will make both parties feel comfortable talking about themselves without asking any direct questions yet."

Don't feel like you must make a good first impression.

Focus on being yourself.

Don't try to be someone you're not.

Don't be afraid of rejection.

Worry about what other people think only if it will help you make them laugh, so long as their laughter isn't at someone else's expense or the result of bullying behavior on their part (e.g., saying something mean behind your back). If someone does say something mean about you in front of others, ignore them and move on with your life. (If it continues, though, tell someone who can help.)

Worry about what others look like - and then forget about it!

Foster positive self-talk before going into a social situation and keep focusing on the positive once you're there.

Positive self-talk is a great way to boost your confidence before starting or continuing a conversation. You can use positive self-talk as you approach the person you want to talk with and after you start talking. Some examples of positive self-talk are:

"This will be easy!"

"I'm going to have fun!"

"People love talking about their hobbies!"

Once you've started talking with the person and find yourself in a comfortable place, remember to focus on the positive aspects of what's happening rather than dwelling on negative thoughts like: "I forgot what she said earlier."

Remember that most people feel just as uncomfortable as you do.

No matter how confident someone looks on the surface, everyone has a moment when they experience social anxiety and don't know what to say. They might be worried about saying something stupid or embarrassing themselves in front of others, just like you are right now! So don't worry about what other people think of you; they probably aren't judging you at all - they've got plenty of their own worries going on too.

By reassuring yourself that everyone else feels nervous sometimes, it's easier to let go of your self-consciousness and start having genuine conversations with strangers.

Use good posture but relax your muscles.

A healthy posture is vital to maintaining good mental health, but there are many who overdo it. You don't need to be always ramrod straight. If a stranger approaches you and asks how your day is going, you're probably not going to be able to think of a witty response while standing up perfectly straight with your arms by your sides. The same goes for speaking on the phone or in front of an audience - if someone asks you a question and you're not sure how to answer, relax! It's okay if they see that you're human just like everyone else.

You'll also want to keep some tension in your muscles as well: if someone walks up and says hello and gives you their hand for shaking, don't let go before they do (even if it feels awkward). Do not cross your arms or give any other indication that this person does not have permission access into whatever personal space bubble he may be extending toward yours; otherwise, he might take offence at being rejected by such an outward display of closed-off-ness/suspicion/hostility/etcetera (see "Jumping Back" below).

Believe in the goodness of others.

One of the biggest hurdles you'll have to get over is believing that people are inherently good. If you're thinking about starting a conversation with a stranger, it's important to know that not everyone is going to be mean or rude. Even though it's easy to assume this when we're anxious, don't let your fear of being hurt keep you from starting conversations with strangers! Use open body language and eye contact to indicate that you are willing to talk.

Use open body language and eye contact to indicate that you are willing to talk.

Keep your hands out of your pockets.

Don't cross your arms, or fidget with anything in your hands (like a cigarette or a book).

Don't look down or away from the person when they are talking to you - instead, make eye contact with them. This will show them that you are interested in what they have to say and that makes it more likely for them to want to keep talking with you as well!

Smile! This is another very important part of communicating effectively with others because it helps put people at ease around us by making them feel comfortable being around us while also allowing us time enough so we can think about what we're going say before actually saying it out loud instead of just blurting out whatever comes first mindlessly without much thought other than just wanting some sort of response right then rather than later as well."

Smile! A genuine smile is contagious, and it also shows that you're an approachable person.

Speak slowly. When you speak slowly and deliberately, you sound more confident - and people are more likely to listen to what you have to say.

Don't be afraid of pauses in conversation; they can make your conversations flow better because they give others a chance to respond more naturally.

Start slowly; avoid conversations with people who are clearly busy or distracted until you're more comfortable starting conversations with strangers in general.

If you're not sure where to begin, start with the people you know. They're a familiar face and they'll usually be happy to see and talk with you.

Avoid starting conversations with people who clearly aren't interested in talking. If someone is busy or distracted, they probably don't want to be bothered by your attempts at conversation. Instead of making them feel awkward by forcing yourself into their space and asking them if they're doing okay/what's going on/why don't we talk about our feelings for once? it's best not to talk at all until the other person shows interest in talking themselves.

The first few times you start conversations with strangers will be nerve-wracking no matter what, so don't worry too much about making a good first impression or what others think of you while doing so (you can always go back later). The only thing that matters during those initial interactions is whether they like talking to you - not whether you liked talking to them!

We hope that these tips helped you to feel more confident about starting conversations with strangers. They are simple tips, but they can make all the difference when it comes to overcoming your social anxiety and improving your ability to connect with people!

THE RISK FACTORS AND SYMPTOMS OF SOCIAL ANXIETY DISORDER

Social anxiety disorder (SAD) is an intense fear of social situations that can make it difficult to function socially. These fears may include anything from speaking in front of a large group to eating or drinking in front of others. The National Institute of Mental Health reports that about 7% of U.S. adults have this type of anxiety disorder at some point in their lives, which means you're not alone if you have them! But since SAD is often misunderstood, here's everything you need to know about what it is, who gets it and how they can manage it:

Social anxiety is a real, diagnosable disorder.

Social anxiety disorder is a real, diagnosable disorder. If you have it, you aren't alone: Social anxiety affects about 15 million people in the United States. It's not a personality or character flaw and it's not just shyness; it's an overwhelming fear of being judged by others. If you have social anxiety disorder, your worries about being watched and judged cause you to avoid everyday activities that other people do without thinking about them (like going to work or school).

Social anxiety is caused by a combination of biological factors (including genetics), environmental stressors (like bullying or trauma) and learned behaviors - it can be difficult to separate one from the others. Some experts believe that the disorder may be caused by an imbalance in brain chemicals called neurotransmitters; however, there isn't enough evidence yet for this theory to be widely accepted.

It's a fear of social situations that allows you to participate normally.

In social anxiety disorder, you fear being watched, judged, and embarrassed in public. You are afraid of looking stupid or saying something that will be embarrassing. This can make it hard to participate normally in social situations.

The symptoms of social anxiety disorder include:

Fear of embarrassment

Fear of being judged or evaluated by others

Fear of acting differently from others

Fear of being watched or talked about negatively by others

Avoiding feared situations can limit your life.

Avoiding feared situations can cause isolation, depression, and loss of important relationships. You may avoid social activities or being in groups that you used to enjoy. This can affect your career and make it harder to get along with people at work.

It's important to remember that what makes you anxious isn't necessarily bad or harmful, but the way you think about it is. If you avoid social situations because of fear, this will keep your anxiety going because it reinforces these fears over time without giving yourself opportunities to overcome them.

People with social anxiety disorder experience overwhelming anxiety and excessive self-consciousness in everyday social situations.

You may be suffering from social anxiety disorder if:

You're afraid of being judged by other people.

You're afraid of being embarrassed in front of others.

You're afraid of being rejected by others.

You're afraid of being humiliated in front of other people.

You're afraid of being belittled or criticized by other people, especially strangers and authority figures (like your boss)

People with extreme social anxiety may worry about being judged by others or being viewed as stupid, awkward, or boring.

People with social anxiety disorder often worry a lot about what other people think of them. They may worry that they will say something stupid or do something embarrassing in front of others. They may also worry that they will look stupid, awkward, or boring.

This is like the way that many people feel when they are at a party. However, for people with social anxiety disorder these feelings can be so strong and overwhelming that it interferes with their daily life on a regular basis.

People with social anxiety disorder often recognize that their fears about being watched or judged are excessive or unreasonable, but they're unable to overcome them.

If you have social anxiety disorder, you may see yourself as a success story - an overachiever who can't seem to win at the game of life. You've earned good grades and gotten into your dream college or graduate program; you have a boyfriend or girlfriend (or both), maybe even kids; yet still, something is missing from your life.

If this sounds familiar, it could be that you suffer from social anxiety disorder (SAD). SAD is a type of anxiety disorder that causes overwhelming feelings of fear and self-doubt in everyday situations like making small talk with strangers or meeting people for the first time. The condition usually starts during adolescence or early adulthood, but symptoms can occur as early as childhood. It affects more than 15 million Americans yearly - one out of every 13 people - yet many don't recognize its symptoms until it's too late to get help.

Fear of embarrassment may lead to feelings of incompetence and low self-esteem.

When you're overcome by the fear of embarrassment, it can lead to avoidance behavior. You may avoid school or work events and activities because you don't want to be judged or embarrassed in front of others. Avoidance might even cause you to drop out of school or quit a job.

The fear of embarrassment can also lead to feelings of shame, guilt and depression. If you think that other people are judging you as incompetent when they look at your face or body language, then chances are good that these negative thoughts will also make their way into your head.

In severe cases, people with social anxiety disorder may become completely isolated and avoid many everyday activities...

In severe cases, people with social anxiety disorder may become completely isolated and avoid many everyday activities. They may also experience a decline in their academic or professional performance.

In some cases, the symptoms of social anxiety disorder can be quite debilitating - so much so that they interfere with your ability to work or go to school, maintain relationships with others, or have fun and participate in life.

According to the National Institute of Mental Health, approximately 7% of U.S. adults have social anxiety disorder at some point in their lives.

Social anxiety disorder is a common mental health concern - it affects approximately 7% of U.S. adults at some point in their lives, according to the National Institute of Mental Health (NIMH). However, social anxiety disorder can be treated with therapy and medication.

The following information will help you understand what social anxiety disorder is and how it's treated:

Women seem to experience more extreme forms of social anxiety than men do...

Women seem to experience more extreme forms of social anxiety than men do, perhaps because they're more likely to have it diagnosed. Women appear to have higher rates of the disorder in general, and they appear to suffer from it over a wider range of situations and activities than their male counterparts do - meaning they may be particularly susceptible to experiencing anxiety at the office or on the bus ride home.

At the same time, however, women may also be less willing than men are to admit that they struggle with any form of mental illness; as such, there are many women who don't seek treatment even though their symptoms interfere with their daily lives. If you think you might be suffering from social anxiety disorder but aren't sure how much it's affecting your life or what kind of help is available for someone like yourself (or if you simply want some advice about getting started), check out our guide below!

Social Anxiety Disorder is real, treatable, and shouldn't be confused with shyness.

Social anxiety disorder is a real, diagnosable anxiety disorder that affects millions of people. It can be treated, but not cured. Social anxiety disorder is characterized by extreme self-consciousness and intense fear of being judged or embarrassed in social settings like parties or public speaking events. People with this condition experience overwhelming anxiety and excessive self-consciousness in everyday social situations; they avoid many social activities, which can significantly limit their ability to maintain normal relationships.

The risk factors and symptoms of social anxiety disorder

The causes of social anxiety are unknown but appear to run in families; if you have a parent who has had similar symptoms over time, you're more likely to develop them yourself. However, there's no clear genetic link between certain genes and susceptibility for developing this condition - which means it may be more complicated than we know yet!

The takeaway is that social anxiety disorder is a real, diagnosable condition. It's treatable, and it doesn't have to rule your life. If you're experiencing symptoms of this condition, seek help from a mental health professional who's experienced in treating social anxiety disorder. You can do it!

HOW TO BE MORE SUCCESSFUL IN YOUR SOCIAL LIFE

Everyone has their own personal definition of success. But, in the simplest terms, success can be defined as living a life that is both happy and meaningful. Having good friends, family and romantic relationships is one way to ensure your life is happy and meaningful. However, it's not always easy to maintain these relationships or build new ones. If you want to be more successful in your social life then here are some tips that will help you achieve just that:

Get out of the house.

You first need to get out of the house and out of your comfort zone. While it may be easy to sit at home and watch Netflix all day, this is not going to help you grow as a person or master social interactions. The best way to do this is by trying new things and seeing what works for you. For example: try different activities like yoga or dance classes, try new restaurants with friends, try new hobbies (like painting or playing sports), or even go on a walk around town! Doing these things regularly, not only will it help keep your mind active but also allow for more opportunities for meeting people!

Work on building connections.

You must work on building connections. This is the foundation of your social life, and it is what will keep you moving forward. If you want to be more successful, then you need to build connections.

It's important to be a good listener and communicate with others effectively - both things are part of being a good friend, which means that they are also essential elements in maintaining your social interactions from a successful perspective.

Stop comparing yourself to others.

You're not comparing your life to others on purpose. It just happens. You see someone with a fancy car, or you go to a party and see everyone having fun but you, and you start thinking "I wish I could have that car too. Or at least be able to socialize like those people."

When this happens, stop telling yourself that it is fine for you not to have what other people have because there are always going to be people who are better than you in some way or another. And yes, I am saying this as someone whose voice has changed three times since I started reading this chapter out loud (I really need more practice).

It's important for us not only on an individual level but also collectively as a society so we don't lose our focus on what matters most: reaching our full potential without caring about what anyone else thinks!

Become more optimistic and positive.

The first step to developing better social skills is becoming more optimistic and positive. This will help you in every aspect of your life, as well as keep you from feeling overwhelmed when you are faced with a challenge or problem. It is also important to accentuate the good in yourself and other people so that you can be happy with who you are right now.

The second step is to learn how to always stay calm even when things get tough which they will at some point! When things don't go the way we want them too we tend to get upset but if we stay calm then those around us will too which means less stress overall!

The third step would be about having courage because without it then everything else won't matter such as being kind towards others because if one person does not have courage then neither does another person therefore there wouldn't be any kindness between each other either."

Learn how to communicate with others.

Listen more than you speak.

Don't interrupt people when they are speaking to you.

Don't talk too much about yourself, unless someone specifically asks you questions about yourself. Instead, ask questions about other people and try to include them in the conversation as much as possible by asking follow-up questions or just listening attentively to what they have to say.

Ask for help with something if you don't know how to do it! It will make you look less clueless and might even give some new skills too!

Saying "I don't know" is fine! If someone asks a question and no one knows the answer, there is nothing wrong with saying that out loud. You may also find that others around have an idea of what the answer could be - so everyone benefits from this kind of exchange of ideas!!

You can do all the things, but success doesn't come without work.

Success is an ongoing process and not an event. It's a journey, not a destination. It's a mindset, not a skill. Success is a habit, not just something you do once in your life and that's it.

Successful people know what they want out of life, and they go after it every single day without fail no matter what obstacles come their way. They know how to maintain their social interactions from a successful perspective because they understand that success takes work!

When it comes down to it, there are no shortcuts to being a successful person in your social life. You can't expect people to like you just because you want them too. You must put in the work and make sure that they do like you. The most important thing is that you get out of the house and try new things - this will help build those connections which will ultimately lead up to a more successful life!

THINGS YOU CAN DO TO IMPROVE YOUR SELF-CONFIDENCE

Confidence is a quality we all want to have. We're also quick to associate it with success and attractiveness. For example, people who have high self-confidence are more likely to succeed at work or get that promotion they've been working toward, while those with low self-confidence often feel unappealing and struggle in relationships. But what exactly is confidence? It's not just about believing in yourself - it's also about believing that others will believe in you as well. And building up that belief can take time! If you're looking for ways to strengthen your own self-confidence, here are some suggestions:

Be realistic and take things in stride.

Be realistic. Don't expect to be perfect and don't compare yourself to others. If you're not confident in a certain area of your life, take steps to improve it rather than beating yourself up about it.

Focus on the positives. When you focus on the negative things that happen in life and allow them to get in the way of your happiness, it's easy for self-confidence issues to develop. Instead, try focusing on all the good things that are happening instead of dwelling on the bad ones – this will help increase confidence over time!

Don't let small things get you down or hold you back from doing what makes you happy.

Give yourself credit for your accomplishments, no matter how small.

Don't be afraid to ask for help when you need it.

Don't compare yourself to others, who may have different goals and circumstances than yours.

Don't be afraid to take risks, even if they don't always pay off - it's better than never trying at all!

And finally: don't be afraid of failure; if something doesn't work out the way you planned it, that doesn't mean it wasn't worth doing in the first place.

Ask others what they see in you.

If you're struggling to develop self-confidence, then it might be time to look at your personality and character traits through someone else's eyes. The problem is that a lot of people have trouble giving themselves positive feedback, so they'll need some help doing so. You can start by asking other people how they see you or your strengths; this is an important first step because it helps put things into perspective for yourself as well. Most importantly, ask them what specific things about yourself are most attractive/appealing/important/etc., because knowing this will make it easier for you to act on those areas once they've been identified (which we'll cover next).

Take care of your appearance.

How you dress can have a huge impact on your feelings of self-confidence. This is because it's one of the main ways that people judge each other, even if they don't realize it. There are a few simple things you can do to make sure that your clothes make you look and feel good:

Know your body type and choose clothing that flatters it. For example, if you're tall and thin, wearing form-fitting clothes will help highlight how tall you are while also making it clear that there isn't much extra weight to hide underneath those clothes. On the other hand, if you're short with more curves than average, baggy clothing might not flatter the way the fabric outlines them instead of hiding them in a flattering way (i.e., unflattering). Choose colors based on what works well with your skin tone rather than what celebrities wear or what's in fashion right now - the latter may not always be flattering for specific skin tones!

Set goals for yourself.

Setting goals is an important step to improving your self-confidence. You can't improve what you can't see, and goals help you to visualize your progress in a way that makes sense to you.

Setting goals is also a great way to stay motivated, as it helps keep you on track and moving towards the things that matter most.

The second reason why setting goals is so important for self-confidence is because it keeps us accountable - we have something concrete on which we can measure our success or failure, which forces us into action when we may otherwise have remained stagnant.

Surround yourself with people who make you feel good about yourself.

You should surround yourself with people who make you feel good about yourself. These are the people who are supportive and honest, who treat you with respect and don't judge you. Surrounding yourself with these kinds of people will help build your self-esteem and confidence because they'll give you positive feedback, which is exactly what we need to grow in our lives and become more successful.

If there's someone in your life right now who doesn't make you feel good about yourself or if there's someone who makes fun of all your accomplishments or makes jokes at your expense, then it's time to distance yourself from this person as soon as possible!

Be the person you want to be.

I'm sure it's obvious, but it's hard to feel confident in yourself if you don't like yourself. And if you don't feel confident in yourself, achieving your goals will be harder. So how can we fix this? We have several options:

Don't compare your life with others' lives (this is important) unless they are doing something that makes them happy and healthy - and even then, try not to compare because everyone's circumstances are different!

Be kind and loving toward yourself! If someone else were harsh or mean toward you, would that make you want to be around them? Probably not!

Try not to judge yourself harshly when trying new things or making mistakes; instead, think of them as learning opportunities!

It takes time to build self-confidence, but it can be done by taking small steps.

You first need to set realistic goals, such as accepting compliments and giving them often. Next, ask others what they see in you that makes them like you and value your opinion. Also, ensure that your appearance is on point by grooming yourself regularly and dressing well for any occasion.

After setting the foundations for building confidence in oneself, it's important for someone who struggles with self-esteem issues (perhaps due to past trauma or other reasons) to consider their own thoughts about themselves and how others perceive them. When we think about our own biases towards ourselves, we may come up with some harsh conclusions:

"I'm too fat/skinny/ugly/bald." However, when we start thinking about what other people say about us or how they treat us in general, those negative thoughts become less valid because they're based on external factors rather than internal ones alone!

As you can see, there are many ways to build self-confidence. It is not something that comes easy for everyone, but if you are willing to put in some work and take it one step at a time, then I think you will be able to improve your level of confidence over time. Remember that this process can take as little as 20 minutes each day, so don't get discouraged if it doesn't work overnight!

DEALING WITH PUBLIC ANXIETY AND OVERCOMING IT.

Anxiety is a normal human emotion, but when it becomes excessive and intrusive, it can be very debilitating. In fact, anxiety disorders affect more than 40 million people in the United States each year. If you have public anxiety (or any other kind of anxiety), then you are certainly not alone! Fortunately for us all, there are plenty of ways to deal with this common problem. Here's how to cope with public anxiety:

Know that you are not alone.

Anxiety is a common human emotion, and it's okay to feel anxious in public.

You're not the only one feeling this way, so don't think you're going crazy or being an outlier for feeling like this!

Don't be ashamed or embarrassed about your anxiety.

It is a normal thing; everyone experiences it from time-to-time. If you are not prepared for it, then it can be embarrassing as well. The best thing you can do is to not let it affect your life or the way you live your life. You can't control your anxiety, but you can control how you react to it and what steps are necessary to overcome public speaking anxiety.

Accept your anxiety for what it is.

Acceptance is the first step to recovery. It's a process, not an event. Acceptance does not mean resignation or giving up; it's an acknowledgement of what is and an acceptance of what can be done. The more you try to fight against your anxiety (by avoiding places that make you anxious), the worse it will get over time -- not just because of what we've talked about so far but also because avoidance reinforces fear-based thinking patterns in the brain.

Distract yourself and focus on the present moment.

Here are some things you can do to help yourself relax:

Focus on what you can see and hear around you. The present moment is real, so focus on it! Your breath, the people around you, and everything else that's happening in this moment - these things will help distract your mind from the anxiety.

Think about something uplifting that happened in the past (a happy memory). If nothing comes to mind right away, think about how grateful you are for certain people or things in your life.

Think about a place that makes you feel calm when thinking about it (your favorite vacation spot). If this doesn't work either, then pick another positive image or thought that gets rid of those feelings from earlier - maybe even something silly like a favorite color or food! This could be anything as long as it's positive and helps bring back those good emotions again!

Learn how to calm yourself down.

To calm yourself down, take deep breaths. Focus on your breathing and slow it down to a rate that feels comfortable. Breathe in through your nose and out through your mouth. If the anxiety continues to be too much, try thinking of something that makes you happy or brings you comfort maybe it's a memory from childhood or a good friend who always makes you laugh. This can help distract you from what's happening right now and make things seem less intense.

If none of this works for reducing your level of anxiety about being in public places, think about someone else who helps give you confidence and trust them as much as possible when dealing with these situations in the future.

Think about what the worst-case scenario would be.

Imagine what would happen if you had a panic attack in public. What could go wrong? What could happen that would be so bad you'd rather not have to deal with it? What would be the worst-case scenario? If you can't think of anything, think about something that is bad but not the end of the world, like getting yelled at by someone for being rude or having a friend ask why you're acting weird. This can help put your fears into perspective and show them for what they are: irrational thoughts that are probably not going to come true - or at least aren't likely enough to warrant letting them control your life.

Think of a backup plan.

If you're having a panic attack, there are many things you can do to help bring it to an end. The first and most important thing is to recognize that you're having an anxiety attack - and that there's nothing wrong with feeling anxious in public.

Once you've recognized what's going on, it's time to find a way out of the situation so that your heart rate can return to normal, and your body can start relaxing again. If possible, try stepping outside for some fresh air or even just sitting down for a few minutes until things get calmer. You could also ask someone to accompany you during this time so they can help keep others away from the area; this will give them something else to focus on instead of whatever is causing these feelings of panic or discomfort in the first place (which means less pressure on yourself).

If none of these work as solutions for reducing anxiety attacks, then consider using self-care techniques such as deep breathing exercises or mindfulness techniques like meditation - both have been shown as effective methods by multiple studies on reducing anxiety levels in patients with panic disorder."

Tell yourself that you are prepared.

You can shift your thinking by telling yourself that you are prepared for whatever might happen. Think about what you have done to prepare for the situation. What have you learned about it? How do you know that everyone else is competent?

Think about how much more comfortable you would be if you were back in your room and able to take a break, as opposed to being out in public with no way to escape an anxious moment.

Remember that you can always leave if you really need to.

If the anxiety is so bad that you can't function, then go home or somewhere else. If the anxiety is bad enough that it's causing physical pain, then go home and see a doctor. If the anxiety is so bad that it's making you feel like vomiting or passing out, then ask someone for help immediately and get yourself checked out by a professional as soon as possible!

It may not be super pleasant to do these things but they are a lot better than having a panic attack in public!

Anxiety is a normal thing, everyone experiences it from time to time.

It's okay to feel anxious as there is nothing shameful about being afraid sometimes.

It's not something to be ashamed of - it's simply part of the human condition and can happen for any number of reasons: from being in an unfamiliar situation, feeling as though you have no control over your environment or simply because you have too much on your plate. The important thing is that we accept our anxiety and allow ourselves to feel it without judgment so that we can move through it more quickly and effectively.

I hope you found this chapter helpful and gave you some ideas on dealing with public anxiety. It is important that we understand those who suffer from these kinds of issues because they are not just strangers on the street but also friends, family members and coworkers too. My goal was to educate people about these conditions to better understand what someone may be going through when they have an anxiety attack in public without making them feel like their experience isn't normal or acceptable!

IMPROVING CONFIDENCE IN SOCIAL SITUATIONS

In this chapter we'll discuss how to improve confidence in social situations. We'll explore some simple tips that will help you feel more confident, such as giving compliments and building meaningful relationships with others. Let's get started!

Give a compliment.

One of the best ways to boost your confidence is to give a compliment. Compliments are a great way to build relationships, and you can use them in any situation, whether it's with someone you know or someone you don't know. The key is making sure the compliment is sincere and specific - not just generic praise like "good job!"

If you want your compliments to be effective, then make sure they focus on something that relates directly back to the person who received it. For example, if their shirt has a cool pattern on it and they love fashion (which most people do), then find something about their outfit that shows off their sense of style.

In addition, make sure not just anyone will do when giving out compliments - choose carefully so that only those who deserve them get one!

Have meaningful conversations.

Having meaningful conversations is one of the best ways to boost your confidence. This is especially true if you're feeling nervous or anxious about social interactions.

There are two main reasons why having meaningful conversations with others will help you feel more confident:

Conversation starters are a helpful tool that can be used in any conversation. They allow you to ease into talking with someone and make them seem more approachable and friendly than they would otherwise be perceived as being. For example, instead of saying "Hi," try asking questions like "How was your weekend?" or "What do you think about this weather?" These types of questions show interest in what another person has to say - and that's one way that people become more interested in us too!

When we engage in meaningful conversations with others (rather than just small talk), we get valuable information about those individuals' lives - and this information often makes them seem much less intimidating! By listening closely when someone else speaks, we learn things about their lives such as their interests and values; this helps us put ourselves at ease when interacting with them even though there may still be some nervousness present at first glance

Don't be afraid of being vulnerable.
If a friend is having a rough time, express your concern and tell them how much you care about them. If you're having a problem, share it with someone who can help you. The more honest and open we are with others, the more likely they will reciprocate this behavior in return.

Making mistakes doesn't make you incompetent or stupid; it shows that you're human! If mistakes aren't harmful in any way (e.g., getting fired from your job), don't let them scare you into hiding from the world forever - go out there and try again! Don't be afraid to ask for help if something seems too difficult for you on your own; no one knows everything by themselves! Lastly, don't be afraid to ask for what YOU want! It might seem scary at first but once again...if we don't try, how will we know?

Take time for self-care.

Self-care is an important part of your overall well-being, and it doesn't have to be expensive or time consuming. Taking a walk around the neighborhood, reading a book on your lunch break, or going to see a movie are all examples of self-care that don't cost much and can boost your confidence.

Of course, some people may need to take things up a notch if their self-esteem is deteriorating or if they suffer from anxiety. The key here is finding activities that you enjoy so that you feel good after doing them - and so do not feel as though they are chores or obligations.

Have an attitude of gratitude.

One of the easiest ways to boost your confidence is by simply being grateful. A gratitude journal is a great way to start; you can write down three things you're grateful for each day, or just list them whenever they occur to you throughout the day.

Even if it's a small thing, like being able to enjoy a sunny spring day or enjoying an interesting book while relaxing at home, remember that there are always things in life worth feeling grateful for!

A little bit of practice can make this attitude come naturally.

Voluntourism is a wonderful way to build connections with others who care about the community and the world we live in.

Volunteering can be a great way to build connections with others who care about the community and world we live in. It's an opportunity to meet people who have similar interests, as well as those who don't, but still care about making a difference. Volunteering can also help you feel more confident when interacting with new people because it gives you experience talking to others about things that matter to them - which will come in handy during interviews or networking events.

Using common sense and maintaining a positive attitude will increase your confidence.

Using common sense and maintaining a positive attitude will increase your confidence. Here are some things to keep in mind:

Don't compare yourself to others, as we all have our own strengths, weaknesses, and experiences.

Be kind to yourself - don't be afraid of making mistakes or being vulnerable, as this is how we learn from our mistakes and grow as people!

Don't be afraid of asking for help when you need it; most people will be more than happy to help another person!

Building confidence is a lifelong process. It can be challenging, but it's worth the effort. You deserve to feel good about yourself! You have so much to offer; the world needs your unique gifts and talents.

HOW TO FEEL COMFORTABLE IN SOCIAL SITUATIONS

I'm a social person. I enjoy going out with friends and meeting new people, but that doesn't mean that every social situation is comfortable for me. I have my fair share of awkward moments where I feel like an outsider or like I'm not saying the right thing. And while these feelings are normal (and often even expected), they don't have to stop you from enjoying yourself in social situations. With some practice, anyone can learn how to work their social powers and make any situation more comfortable for themselves!

Fake it till you make it.

The best way to convince yourself that you are confident and relaxed is to pretend that you are. When you start feeling anxious, act like a confident person would act. Smile and laugh at jokes, even if they aren't particularly funny. Don't be afraid of making small talk with strangers; it's a great way to meet new people! If someone asks about your job or hobbies, answer them honestly - but don't let any negative emotions show on your face or in your voice.

When we're feeling nervous, our body language tends to communicate anxiety: crossed arms and legs indicate discomfort; facial expressions betray fear or uneasiness; voices may pitch higher than normal when we speak. Try not to let these things happen - fake the confidence until it becomes real!

Be prepared.

In order to be prepared, you must be able to answer questions in a way that makes you look good. For example, if someone asks you what your favorite movie is, don't say something like "I don't know." Instead, choose one of the following three responses:

"My favorite movie is ___ because it's so funny/inspiring/etc.! Have you seen it? It's on Netflix."

"I'm not sure what my favorite movie is but I love the character development in ____."

"That's a tough question! How about we go watch one together sometime?"

Take a deep breath.

One of the best ways to deal with social anxiety is taking a deep breath. Breathing exercises can help you relax, focus, and even manage stress. It's not just about breathing; it's also about how long you take that breath in and how much air you fill your lungs with. If you are feeling anxious or panicky, try taking a few slow breaths through your nose while counting to five to regulate yourself before going into the situation.

Take a deep breath in through your nose for 4 seconds

Hold for 2 seconds

Exhale through pursed lips for 4 seconds

Be positive.

We all know someone negative. It's impossible to be around this person for more than a few minutes and not feel the negativity seep into your mood. The same holds when you're in social situations. If you're focused on complaining, there's little chance that people will enjoy being around you or want to interact with you. By contrast, if your focus is on what can be done for others or how we can help each other - rather than focusing on the negative aspects of life - you'll feel much more positive about yourself and others.

Focus on your strengths.

The first thing to do is focus on your strengths. You may not be the best at everything, but you can do something well! There are many different things you're good at, and it's vital that you recognise and celebrate them. Try to spend some time doing something that makes you feel good about yourself daily. This can be anything from working out to reading a book or writing in your journal, so long as it helps build confidence in your abilities and allows for self-expression.

Another way to feel more comfortable is by not worrying about what other people think of you all the time! Everyone has their own opinions, but they don't know anything about who we are; if someone doesn't like us for reasons utterly unrelated to their own lives, then we shouldn't waste our time worrying about what they think anyway! Be confident in who

Focus on the positive qualities in others.

The key to having a great time is to focus on those around you. It's easy to get caught up in the nitty-gritty of your own life, but it's much more fun if you can put yourself in other people's shoes and tune into what they're going through. The best way to do this is by focusing on the good things about them, not their flaws or shortcomings - even if those things are glaringly obvious! For example: "She has terrible breath!" could become "She's an awesome kisser!" If she doesn't smell good, maybe she hasn't had time for hygiene yet. Or maybe she was eating onions earlier? Instead of making assumptions or being critical, try thinking positively about others instead!

In social situations, focus on what you offer and not your weaknesses.

Feeling insecure makes it easy to focus on what you don't have or aren't good at. However, when you start focusing on your strengths and the positive qualities in others, it helps you be more confident and comfortable in social situations.

When preparing yourself for a social situation where there is likely to be some anxiety involved, consider what strengths or resources are available to help reduce that anxiety. How can those strengths be used? Can any of these ideas work for other types of social situations?

Focusing on your strengths to be more comfortable in social situations. You can also fake it till you make it by pretending like everything is okay, even when it isn't. Focusing on others will help them feel comfortable in their skin too!

THE AUTHOR

Chloe is a middle-aged local activist who enjoys helping old ladies across the road, fitness, and human psychology. She is energetic and giving but can also be cowardly and untidy. She has a degree in philosophy, politics, and economics. She is allergic to milk (go figure). She grew up in a middle-class neighbourhood. She was raised by her father, her mother having left when she was young. Since her early teen years, Chloe has been fascinated by the psychology of the human mind and all the journeys it takes people on. Being a non-confronting pacifist wrapped in an empathetic blanket, Chloe has always experienced the power of her mind in the most exciting combinations imaginable.